# Breakfast bowls

Caroline
Griffiths

# Breakfast bowls

52 nourishing recipes
to kick-start your day

Smith
Street
Books

# Contents

# Introduction

Beginning your morning with a beautiful breakfast is the best way to set the tone for a day full of possibility and even greater things to come. Breakfast, as they say, is the most important meal of the day – it's certainly the most interesting and adaptable – and the natural beauty of the breakfast bowls within these pages is sure to get your day off to a great start.

This book provides plenty of options for leisurely breakfasts, as well as ideas for meals that you can prepare ahead of time, take from the fridge as you walk out the door and enjoy when you get to work. The only thing you'll need is your favourite bowl so you can enjoy your breakfast to the full.

## Special tips for smoothie bowls

The smoothie bowl recipes in this book all serve two, as this is the maximum amount of ingredients most blenders can hold. If you only need to make one serve, it is easy to halve the recipes and freeze any leftover smoothie mixture in popsicle moulds or ice cube trays. Or you can multiply the recipe if feeding more, and blend in batches.

Keep your freezer stocked with peeled chopped fruit so you can whiz up a smoothie bowl whenever you like. If you don't have frozen fruit, don't panic, your smoothie bowl just won't be as thick. You can add extra crushed ice to thicken.

You will need a high-speed blender or food processor to effectively make a smoothie bowl. The smoothie should be thick and luscious – remember you want to be able to scoop it with a spoon, not drink it through a straw.

## Notes on ingredients

### Acai

Available from wholefood stores, typically in either frozen pulp (purée) or berry form, or as a powdered supplement. You can substitute frozen acai pulp with frozen berries of your choice (blueberries or raspberries work well) mixed with 1–2 tablespoons of acai powder.

### Bee pollen

This protein-rich food is available in granular, powdered and capsule forms from health food stores. I use the granular bee pollen.

### Bonito flakes (katsuobushi)

Smoked bonito or skipjack tuna that has been fermented and dried, then shaved very finely.

### Cacao nibs

The dried and fully fermented seed of the cacao plant. Cacao nibs have a great chocolatey punch, a fantastic crunch and a slight bitterness. Available from health food stores and selected supermarkets.

**Carob powder**

A ground legume with a mild chocolate flavour with caramel undertones. Available from health food stores and good supermarkets.

**Coconut yoghurt**

A rich, cultured, non-dairy alternative to traditional yoghurt. It is available in health food stores and good supermarkets.

**Dragon fruit (pitaya)**

A spectacular fruit indigenous to the Americas and widely grown in Asia. Buy fresh when in season, otherwise dragon fruit is available frozen from good health food stores. I find the pink-fleshed variety more fragrant than the white.

**Edible flowers**

You can use your own edible flowers from your garden – if you know they are unsprayed and you have grown them from seed – or purchase fresh in punnets from good green grocers. Popular edible flowers include rose petals, marigolds, nasturtiums, violas and pea flowers and edible dried flowers include rose buds and petals and lavender flowers. Available from gourmet food stores.

**Inca berries**

Also known as cape gooseberries, inca berries are indigenous to South America and are most commonly available dried. They have a golden bronze colour with small edible crunchy seeds. They are high in fibre and antioxidants.

**Milk, milk kefir and milk alternatives**

Unless specified, recipes use dairy milk or milk kefir. Kefir is a cultured milk with a tangy flavour and thin yoghurt-like consistency that you can make yourself or purchase from health food stores. Non-dairy alternatives are numerous and include almond, rice, oat, soy and coconut milks. Choose the milk alternative that will best suit your nutritional needs.

**Millet, hulled**

Millet is a tiny round cereal grain thought to have originated in western Africa. The grains have a mild buttery taste that is enhanced by toasting before cooking. Available from health food stores.

**Powdered supplements**

Green superfoods powder is a combination of spirulina, chlorella and wheatgrass and is available from health food stores. There are a number of variations available, choose one to suit your needs.

**Protein powder**

There are many different types of protein powders available but most consist of protein from soy, pea or dairy (whey or casein). For an extra boost, add a tablespoon of protein powder to any smoothie bowl.

### Rice malt syrup

Made by culturing rice with enzymes to break down the starches, and then cooking down to create a thick syrup. Rice malt syrup has a similar texture to honey but is less sweet on the palate. It is available from health food stores and supermarkets.

## Notes on toppings and garnishes

### Balled fruit

Cut the fruit in half, scoop out any seeds if necessary, then sink the edge of a melon baller into the fruit and rotate the edge all the way around to make a perfect sphere.

### Citrus rind strips

Peel 1.5 cm (½ in) wide strips from the fruit with a vegetable peeler, remove the white pith with a small sharp knife and cut into long thin strips. Save the fruit once you have removed the rind.

### Citrus segments

Using a sharp knife, carefully slice off the top and bottom of the fruit. Slice the skin from the flesh and remove any remaining white pith. Holding the fruit in one hand over a bowl to catch the juice, carefully slice between the membranes to separate the segments.

### Toasted flaked coconut or almonds

Preheat the oven to 160°C/320°F (fan-forced). Spread flaked coconut or almonds on a baking paper-lined baking tray and bake for 4–5 minutes or until golden and fragrant. Set aside to cool.

### Toasted nuts

Preheat the oven to 160°C/320°F (fan-forced). Spread nuts on a baking paper-lined baking tray and bake for 8-10 minutes or until golden and fragrant. Set aside to cool.

### Crushed toasted sesame seeds

Preheat the oven to 160°C/320°F (fan-forced). Spread sesame seeds on a baking paper-lined baking tray and bake for 5–8 minutes or until lightly browned. Set aside to cool. Using a mortar and pestle, lightly crush the sesame seeds with a pinch of salt.

### Spiralised zucchini (courgette)

If you have a spiraliser, use according to the manufacturer's instuctions. If you don't have a spiralising tool, slice the zucchini very thinly lengthways with a sharp knife or a mandoline. Stack the slices on top of each other and then cut into long thin strips.

## Notes on dietary definitions

### Refined sugar-free

These recipes do not contain refined white or brown cane (or beet) sugar.

### Vegetarian

These recipes do not contain meat or fish.

### Vegan

These recipes do not contain any animal products. Vegan recipes are all vegetarian and dairy-free.

### Dairy free

These recipes do not contain products made with cow's milk, such as butter, milk, yoghurt and cheese.

### Gluten free

These recipes are free from the grains that contain the protein gluten. I have not included oats in this classification, and have listed tamari as a gluten-free alternative when soy sauce is required.

### Grain free

These recipes do not contain grains of any form, including oats, rice, wheat, corn and barley.

## Notes on measurements and cooking

### Measurements

All cup and spoon measures are level and based on metric measures.

- 1 cup = 250 ml/8½ fl oz
- 1 tablespoon = 20 ml/¾ fl oz/4 teaspoons

### Ovens

All oven temperatures are fan-forced. To convert to a conventional oven temperature, increase the temperature by about 20°C (70°F) or check the oven manufacturer's instructions.

# Smoothie bowls

Acai (pronounced *a-sigh-ee*) berries are a Brazilian superfood high in antioxidants. The fruit comes from a palm tree and resembles blueberries in appearance. Acai is available from health food stores, in either frozen pulp (purée) or berry form, or as a powder.

# Acai smoothie bowl with crunchy granola

125 g (4½ oz/½ cup) natural yoghurt or 125 ml (4 fl oz/½ cup) milk kefir

40 g (1½ oz/⅓ cup) crushed ice

2 peeled bananas, frozen and roughly chopped

200 g (7 oz) frozen unsweetened acai berry pulp, broken up

1 tablespoon chia seeds (optional)

lime juice, to taste

honey, to taste (optional)

**To serve**

Crunchy citrus toasted granola (page 48)

fresh figs

pomegranate seeds

shaved Brazil nuts

edible flowers

honey (optional)

Whiz the yoghurt or kefir with the ice, banana, acai pulp and chia seeds (if using) in a high-speed blender or small food processor until smooth. Scrape down the inside of the blender or processor bowl if required. If the mixture isn't moving well in the blender, add a tablespoon or two of water or kefir, being careful not to add too much liquid.

Taste the smoothie and add a squeeze of lime juice and a drizzle of honey (if necessary) to balance the flavour to your liking.

Spoon the thick smoothie mixture immediately into two chilled bowls and top with granola, figs, pomegranate, Brazil nuts and flowers. If you like, finish with a drizzle of honey.

**Makes 2**

**Refined-sugar free | Vegetarian | Gluten free | Grain free**

*To make **dairy free**, replace the yoghurt or milk with a non-dairy alternative. To make **vegan**, also swap the honey for rice malt syrup, pure maple syrup or a couple of drops of liquid stevia.*

# Carob & almond brownie smoothie bowl

60 g (2 oz/½ cup) crushed ice

2 peeled bananas, frozen and roughly chopped

25 g (1 oz/¼ cup) carob powder

1 tablespoon chia seeds (optional)

125 ml (4 fl oz/½ cup) unsweetened almond milk

honey, to taste

## Caramelised almonds and honey

20 g (¾ oz/¼ cup) flaked almonds

1 tablespoon sesame seeds

1 tablespoon honey

## To serve

chopped banana

edible flowers

bee pollen

honey (optional)

To make the caramelised almonds and honey, heat the almonds and sesame seeds in a small frying pan over medium heat. Cook for 2–3 minutes or until golden and fragrant. Add the honey and cook for a further 2–3 minutes, stirring and shaking the pan constantly, until the mixture is well coated and the honey starts to darken slightly in colour. Spread onto a baking paper-lined baking tray and set aside to cool. Break into pieces.

Whiz the ice, banana, carob powder, chia seeds (if using) and almond milk in a high-speed blender or small food processor until smooth. Scrape down the inside of the blender or processor bowl if required. If the mixture isn't moving well in the blender, add a tablespoon or two of water or almond milk, being careful not to add too much liquid.

Taste the smoothie and add a drizzle of honey to adjust the sweetness to your liking.

Spoon the thick smoothie mixture immediately into two chilled bowls and top with banana, the caramelised almonds, flowers and a sprinkling of bee pollen. If you like, finish with a drizzle of honey.

**Makes 2**

**Refined-sugar free | Vegetarian | Dairy free | Gluten free | Grain free**

*To make **vegan**, swap the honey for rice malt syrup, pure maple syrup or a couple of drops of liquid stevia and leave out the bee pollen.*

Carob has a mild chocolate flavour with caramel undertones. Combined with almond milk here, it's like a chocolate brownie in smoothie form. Carob powder is available from good health food stores and some supermarkets.

This bowl was inspired by my travels in Vietnam, where avocado is often used in delicious smoothies. Avocado is an intriguing and totally underrated 'sweet' ingredient. Here it lends a lovely silky texture and great nutty flavour.

# Avocado & matcha smoothie bowl

125 ml (4 fl oz/½ cup) tinned coconut milk or coconut water

60 g (2 oz/½ cup) crushed ice

2 peeled bananas, frozen and roughly chopped

1 avocado, stone removed

2½ teaspoons matcha (green tea) powder

1 teaspoon natural vanilla extract

pinch of sea salt flakes

lime juice, to taste

honey, to taste

### To serve

sliced or cubed avocado

flaked coconut or shaved fresh coconut

raw cacao nibs

lime wedges

mint leaves

Whiz the coconut milk or water with the ice, banana, avocado, matcha powder and vanilla extract in a high-speed blender or small food processor until smooth. Scrape down the inside of the blender or processor bowl if required. If the mixture isn't moving well in the blender, add a tablespoon or two of water or milk, being careful not to add too much liquid.

Taste the smoothie and add a pinch of salt, a squeeze of lime juice and a drizzle of honey to balance the flavour to your liking.

Spoon the thick smoothie mixture immediately into two chilled bowls and top with avocado, coconut, cacao nibs, lime wedges and a few mint leaves.

### Makes 2

**Refined-sugar free | Vegetarian | Dairy free | Gluten free | Grain free**

*To make vegan, swap the honey for rice malt syrup, pure maple syrup or a couple of drops of liquid stevia.*

# Banana–berrylicious smoothie bowl

125 g (4½ oz/½ cup) natural yoghurt or 125 ml (4 fl oz/½ cup) milk kefir

60 g (2 oz/½ cup) crushed ice

2 peeled bananas, frozen and roughly chopped

120 g (4½ oz/¾ cup) frozen mixed berries

1 tablespoon chia seeds (optional)

honey, to taste

### To serve

Cacao and black tahini granola (page 51)

sliced banana rolled in shredded coconut

fresh berries

Whiz the yoghurt or kefir with the ice, banana, berries and chia seeds (if using) in a high-speed blender or small food processor until smooth. Scrape down the inside of the blender or processor bowl if required. If the mixture isn't moving well in the blender, add a tablespoon or two of water or kefir, being careful not to add too much liquid.

Taste the smoothie and add a drizzle of honey to adjust the sweetness to your liking.

Spoon the thick smoothie mixture immediately into two chilled bowls and top with the granola, banana and berries.

**Makes 2**

**Refined-sugar free** | **Vegetarian** | **Gluten free** | **Grain free**

*To make **dairy free**, replace the yoghurt or milk with a non-dairy alternative. To make **vegan**, also swap the honey for rice malt syrup, pure maple syrup or a couple of drops of liquid stevia.*

Use fresh berries instead of frozen when they are in season and abundant. This smoothie bowl is great to whip up on short notice as it uses simple ingredients that you are likely to already have stocked in your house.

The earthiness of the beetroot (beets) in this smoothie bowl is tempered by the natural sweetness of the apple, and the lemon slices give it a wonderful kick. This smoothie bowl will be a little less thick than most of the others – if you want it slightly thicker, freeze the chopped beetroot.

# Beetroot, banana & apple smoothie bowl

125 g (4½ oz/½ cup)
 natural yoghurt or 125 ml
 (4 fl oz/½ cup) milk kefir
60 g (2 oz/½ cup) crushed
 ice
1 peeled banana, frozen
 and roughly chopped
1 small beetroot (beet),
 scrubbed or peeled and
 roughly chopped
1 apple, cored and roughly
 chopped
2 slices lemon (skin on)

**To serve**
natural yoghurt
Coconut, sesame and
 matcha clusters
 (page 52)
raw cacao nibs

Whiz the yoghurt or kefir with the ice, banana, beetroot, apple and lemon slices in a high-speed blender or small food processor until smooth. Scrape down the inside of the blender or processor bowl if required. If the mixture isn't moving well in the blender, add a tablespoon or two of water or kefir, being careful not to add too much liquid.

Spoon the thick smoothie mixture immediately into two chilled bowls and top with a swirl of yoghurt. Scatter with the coconut, sesame and matcha clusters and a sprinkle of cacao nibs.

**Makes 2**

**Refined-sugar free | Vegetarian | Gluten free | Grain free**

*To make **vegan**, replace the yoghurt and/or kefir with a non-dairy alternative.*

# Blueberry muffin smoothie bowl

250 g (9 oz/1 cup) natural yoghurt or 250 ml (8½ fl oz/1 cup) milk kefir

60 g (2 oz/½ cup) crushed ice

2 peeled bananas, frozen and roughly chopped

150 g (5½ oz/1 cup) frozen blueberries

1 tablespoon ground linseed (flaxseed meal)

1 teaspoon natural vanilla extract

freshly squeezed lime juice, to taste

honey, to taste

### To serve

natural yoghurt

sliced banana

fresh blueberries, freeze-dried and/or dried blueberries

dried mulberries

activated buckwheat

edible flowers

Whiz the yoghurt or kefir with the ice, banana, blueberries, linseed and vanilla extract in a high-speed blender or small food processor until smooth. Scrape down the inside of the blender or processor bowl if required. If the mixture isn't moving well in the blender, add a tablespoon or two of water or kefir, being careful not to add too much liquid.

Taste the smoothie and add a squeeze of lime juice and a drizzle of honey to balance the flavour to your liking.

Spoon the thick smoothie mixture immediately into two chilled bowls and top with a swirl of yoghurt. Scatter with the banana, berries, buckwheat and flowers.

**Makes 2**

**Refined-sugar free | Vegetarian | Gluten free | Grain free**

*To make **dairy free**, replace the yoghurt and/or milk kefir with a non-dairy alternative. To make **vegan**, also swap the honey for rice malt syrup, pure maple syrup or a couple of drops of liquid stevia.*

Blueberries are little nutritional powerhouses. They are the star feature of this vibrant smoothie, which uses fresh and freeze-dried berries. Each style adds its own texture and variation on blueberry flavour. Freeze-dried blueberries are available from good health food stores and some supermarkets.

This smoothie bowl takes the classic combo of chocolate and hazelnut to the next level – and makes it healthier along the way. A blender will give you a smoother hazelnut butter (and nut butter in general) than a food processor. Try adding some ground cardamom or ginger for a twist.

# Choc–hazelnut smoothie bowl

60 g (2 oz/½ cup) crushed ice

2 frozen peeled bananas, roughly chopped

125 ml (4 fl oz/½ cup) unsweetened almond milk

honey, to taste

**Choc–hazelnut butter**

280 g (10 oz/2 cups) hazelnuts

4 fresh (medjool) dates, seeded and chopped

25 g (1 oz/¼ cup) raw cacao powder

1 teaspoon natural vanilla extract

80 ml (2 fl oz/¼ cup) drinking coconut milk, plus more if required

pinch of sea salt flakes

**To serve**

Cacao and black tahini granola (page 51)

chopped toasted hazelnuts (see page 8)

edible flowers

To make the choc–hazelnut butter, preheat the oven to 160°C/320°F (fan-forced). Line a baking tray with non-stick baking paper and cover with the hazelnuts in a single layer. Roast for 5–8 minutes or until the skins have loosened. Cool slightly then rub the hazelnuts in a clean kitchen towel to remove the skins. Whiz the warm hazelnuts in a high-speed blender or food processor until very finely chopped. Add the dates and whiz again until combined. Then, add the cacao, vanilla extract, coconut milk and salt, and blend until the mixture is quite smooth and buttery (be patient, it could take up to 10 minutes, depending on your appliance). Scrape down the inside of the blender or processor bowl and add a little more coconut milk if required. This recipe makes about 450 g (1 lb/1½ cups). Store in an airtight container in the refrigerator for up to 2 weeks.

Whiz the ice, banana and almond milk with 100 g (3½ oz/⅓ cup) of the choc–hazelnut butter in a high-speed blender or small food processor until smooth. Scrape down the inside of the blender or processor bowl if required. If the mixture isn't moving well in the blender, add a tablespoon or two of water or milk, being careful not to add too much liquid.

Spoon the thick smoothie mixture immediately into two chilled bowls and top with granola, hazelnuts, edible flowers and an extra dollop or two of the hazelnut butter.

**Makes 2**

**Refined-sugar free | Vegetarian | Dairy free | Gluten free | Grain free**

*To make **vegan**, swap the honey for rice malt syrup, pure maple syrup or a couple of drops of liquid stevia.*

# Carrot cake smoothie bowl

250 g (9 oz/1 cup) natural yoghurt or 250 ml (8½ fl oz/1 cup) milk kefir

60 g (2 oz/½ cup) crushed ice

2 carrots, grated

160 g (2 oz/1 cup) pineapple cubes, frozen

1 peeled orange, chopped and frozen

1 peeled banana, frozen and roughly chopped

2 thin slices lemon (skin on)

2 teaspoons vanilla extract

2 teaspoons ground cinnamon

½ teaspoon finely grated fresh ginger

pinch of nutmeg

honey, to taste (optional)

**To serve**

julienned carrot

toasted walnuts (see page 8)

toasted pepitas (pumpkin seeds)

flaked coconut

ground cinnamon

Whiz the yoghurt or kefir with the ice, carrot, pineapple, orange, banana, lemon, vanilla extract, cinnamon, ginger and nutmeg in a high-speed blender or small food processor until smooth. Scrape down the inside of the blender or processor bowl if required. If the mixture isn't moving well in the blender, add a tablespoon or two of water or kefir, being careful not to add too much liquid.

Taste the smoothie and, if necessary, add a drizzle of honey to adjust the sweetness to your liking.

Spoon the thick smoothie mixture immediately into two chilled bowls and top with the carrot, walnuts, pepitas and coconut, and sprinkle with cinnamon.

**Makes 2**

**Refined-sugar free | Vegetarian | Gluten free | Grain free**

*To make **dairy free**, replace the yoghurt or milk kefir with a non-dairy alternative. To make **vegan**, also swap the honey for rice malt syrup, pure maple syrup or a couple of drops of liquid stevia.*

This smoothie bowl is like a cross between a carrot cake and a hummingbird cake – who says you can't eat cake for breakfast?

Dragon fruit (pitaya) is a spectacular and unusual-looking fruit. Look for it fresh when it's in season, otherwise you can buy it frozen from good health food stores. The seeds have a lovely crunchy texture that contrasts with the juicy flesh. I find the pink-fleshed variety more fragrant than the white and it will give a more vibrant colour to your smoothie bowl.

# Dragon fruit & watermelon smoothie bowl

125 ml (4 fl oz/½ cup) tinned coconut milk or 125 g (4½ oz/½ cup) coconut yoghurt

60 g (2 oz/½ cup) crushed ice

1 peeled pink or white dragon fruit (pitaya), chopped and frozen

135 g (5 oz/1 cup) watermelon cubes, frozen

1 peeled banana, frozen and roughly chopped

honey, to taste

**To serve**

Cacao and black tahini granola (page 51)

cubed dragon fruit

sliced starfruit (carambola)

Whiz the coconut milk or yoghurt with the ice, dragon fruit, watermelon and banana in a high-speed blender or small food processor until smooth. Scrape down the inside of the blender or processor bowl if required. If the mixture isn't moving well in the blender, add a tablespoon or two of water or milk, being careful not to add too much liquid.

Taste the smoothie and add a drizzle of honey to adjust the sweetness to your liking.

Spoon the thick smoothie mixture immediately into two chilled bowls and top with granola, dragon fruit and starfruit.

**Makes 2**

**Refined-sugar free | Vegetarian | Dairy free | Gluten free | Grain free**

*To make **vegan**, swap the honey for rice malt syrup, pure maple syrup or a couple of drops of liquid stevia.*

# Mango & turmeric lassi smoothie bowl

125 g (4½ oz/½ cup) natural yoghurt

60 g (2 oz/½ cup) crushed ice

1 mango, flesh chopped and frozen

2 peeled bananas, frozen and roughly chopped

juice and pulp of 1 orange

1 tablespoon finely grated fresh turmeric or 2 teaspoons ground turmeric

¼ teaspoon finely grated fresh ginger

lemon juice, to taste

honey, to taste (optional)

**To serve**

sliced mango

shredded dried mango

mint leaves

toasted flaked almonds (see page 8)

Whiz the yoghurt, ice, mango, banana, orange juice and pulp, turmeric and ginger in a high-speed blender or small food processor until smooth. Scrape down the inside of the blender or processor bowl if required. If the mixture isn't moving well in the blender, add a tablespoon or two of water or milk, being careful not to add too much liquid.

Taste the smoothie and add a squeeze of lemon juice and a drizzle of honey (if necessary) to balance the flavour to your liking.

Spoon the thick smoothie mixture immediately into two chilled bowls and top with the fresh and dried mango, mint and almonds.

**Makes 2**

**Refined-sugar free | Vegetarian | Gluten free | Grain free**

*To make **dairy free**, replace the yoghurt with a non-dairy alternative.*
*To make **vegan**, also swap the honey for rice malt syrup, pure maple syrup or a couple of drops of liquid stevia.*

This refreshing, summery smoothie is like a thick Indian lassi, with a few more tasty and healthful ingredients added for good measure. When mangoes are in season, at their best and most economical to buy, I chop them into cubes and freeze in zip-lock bags.

This is a recipe for the height of summer. Make the most of peaches, nectarines, plums and cherries as soon as they are available. One of the delights of seasonality is enjoying produce when it is available from local suppliers – not only are you supporting local farmers, the produce will be packed with nutrition and flavour.

# Summer stone fruit smoothie bowl

125 g (4½ oz/½ cup) natural yoghurt or 125 ml (4 fl oz/½ cup) milk kefir

60 g (2 oz/½ cup) crushed ice

2 peeled bananas, frozen and roughly chopped

2 peaches, nectarines or plums, stones removed

1 tablespoon chia seeds (optional)

honey or pure maple syrup, to taste

**To serve**

thinly sliced stone fruit

pitted cherries

flaked almonds

edible flowers

Whiz the yoghurt or kefir with the ice, fruit and chia seeds (if using) in a high-speed blender or small food processor until smooth. Scrape down the inside of the blender or processor bowl if required. If the mixture isn't moving well in the blender, add a tablespoon or two of water or kefir, being careful not to add too much liquid.

Taste the smoothie and add a drizzle of honey or maple syrup to adjust the sweetness to your liking.

Spoon the thick smoothie mixture immediately into two chilled bowls and top with the stone fruit, cherries, almonds and flowers.

**Makes 2**

**Refined-sugar free | Vegetarian | Gluten free | Grain free**

*To make **dairy free**, replace the yoghurt or milk kefir with a non-dairy alternative. To make **vegan**, also swap the honey for rice malt syrup, pure maple syrup or a couple of drops of liquid stevia.*

# Tropical paradise smoothie bowl

250 g (9 oz/1 cup) coconut yoghurt or 250 ml (8½ fl oz/1 cup) coconut kefir

1 mango, flesh chopped and frozen

150 g (5½ oz/1 cup) frozen chopped pineapple

1 peeled banana, frozen and roughly chopped

1 tablespoon shredded fresh mint leaves

1 tablespoon chia seeds (optional)

1 tablespoon lime juice, or to taste

**To serve**

passionfruit pulp

balled gold and green kiwi fruit and pink dragon fruit (pitaya) (see page 8)

roughly chopped macadamia nuts

mint leaves

shredded lime zest

Whiz the yoghurt or kefir with the mango, pineapple, banana, mint leaves and chia seeds (if using) in a high-speed blender or small food processor until smooth. Scrape down the inside of the blender or processor bowl if required. If the mixture isn't moving well in the blender, add a tablespoon or two of water or coconut milk, being careful not to add too much liquid.

Taste the smoothie and add a squeeze of lime juice to balance the flavour to your liking.

Spoon the thick smoothie mixture immediately into two chilled bowls and top with the passionfruit, kiwi fruit, dragon fruit, macadamia nuts, mint leaves and lime zest.

**Makes 2**

**Refined-sugar free | Vegan | Gluten free | Grain free**

Start your day transported to an island holiday with this vibrant and refreshing smoothie bowl. The dragonfruit adds a bold magenta to this colourful bowl of joy.

Packed with green power, this smoothie will get you firing on all cylinders! Green superfoods powder is a combination of spirulina, chlorella and wheatgrass – available from health food stores and some supermarkets. Other superfoods powders will work well in this recipe too. Try maca, acai, mesquite or protein powder.

# Supergreens smoothie bowl

250 g (9 oz/1 cup) natural yoghurt or 250 ml (8½ fl oz/1 cup) milk kefir

60 g (2 oz/½ cup) crushed ice

3 handfuls baby spinach leaves or shredded kale

1 avocado, stone removed

2 tablespoons mint leaves

1 tablespoon ground linseed (flaxseed meal)

1 tablespoon green superfoods powder

lime juice, to taste

honey, to taste

**To serve**

cubed avocado

pepitas (pumpkin seeds)

hemp seeds

mint leaves

Whiz the yoghurt or kefir with the ice, spinach or kale and the avocado, mint, linseed and superfoods powder in a high-speed blender or small food processor until smooth. Scrape down the inside of the blender or processor bowl if required. If the mixture isn't moving well in the blender, add a tablespoon or two of water or kefir, being careful not to add too much liquid.

Taste the smoothie and add a squeeze of lime juice and a drizzle of honey to balance the flavour to your liking.

Spoon the thick smoothie mixture immediately into two chilled bowls and top with the avocado, pepitas, hemp seeds and mint.

**Makes 2**

**Refined-sugar free | Vegetarian | Gluten free | Grain free**

*To make **dairy free**, replace the yoghurt or kefir with a non-dairy alternative. To make **vegan**, also swap the honey for rice malt syrup, pure maple syrup or a couple of drops of liquid stevia.*

# Vanilla super protein smoothie bowl

250 g (9 oz/1 cup) natural yoghurt or 250 ml (8½ fl oz/1 cup) milk kefir

60 g (2 oz/½ cup) crushed ice

2 peeled bananas, frozen and roughly chopped

2 tablespoons vanilla whey protein isolate powder

1 tablespoon chia seed oil

2 teaspoons natural vanilla extract

honey, to taste (optional)

**To serve**

Cacao and black tahini granola (page 51)

blueberries

bee pollen

Whiz the yoghurt or kefir with the ice, banana, whey powder, oil and vanilla extract in a high-speed blender or small food processor until smooth. Scrape down the inside of the blender or processor bowl if required. If the mixture isn't moving well in the blender, add a tablespoon or two of water or kefir, being careful not to add too much liquid.

Taste the smoothie and, if necessary, add a drizzle of honey to adjust the sweetness to your liking.

Spoon the thick smoothie mixture immediately into two chilled bowls and top with granola, blueberries and bee pollen.

**Makes 2**

**Refined-sugar free | Vegetarian | Gluten free | Grain free**

*To make **dairy free**, replace the yoghurt or milk kefir with a non-dairy alternative and use a pea protein powder instead of the whey protein isolate. To make **vegan**, also swap the honey for rice malt syrup, pure maple syrup or a couple of drops of liquid stevia, and leave out the bee pollen.*

This smoothie bowl is a full-on protein hit, great before heading to the gym or to help with recovery after a tough workout. For an extra boost, add a couple of teaspoons of maca, acai or mesquite powder with the whey protein.

# Seed & grain bowls

Chia pudding keeps well in the refrigerator for three to four days, so it's great to make a batch and enjoy it over the week. I particularly like to use black chia seeds as the colour works well with the white coconut – though white seeds will be fine if that's all you have.

# Coconut & lime chia pudding bowl

60 g (2 oz/⅓ cup) chia seeds

1 teaspoon finely grated lime zest

200 ml (7 fl oz) tinned coconut milk

200 ml (7 fl oz) fresh or unsweetened coconut water

lime juice, to taste

**To serve**
fresh berries
shaved fresh or dried coconut
edible flowers
shredded lime zest

Combine the chia seeds, lime zest, coconut milk and coconut water in a small bowl. Cover and refrigerate for at least 1–2 hours or overnight, stirring occasionally, until thickened. If the pudding becomes too thick, thin with a little water, coconut milk or coconut water to the consistency you like.

Taste the pudding and add a squeeze of lime juice to balance the flavour to your liking.

Serve the chia pudding into bowls and top with berries, coconut, flowers and shredded lime zest.

**Makes 4**

**Refined-sugar free | Vegan | Gluten free | Grain free**

# Choc–gingerbread chia pudding bowl

1 apple or pear (skin on), grated

60 g (2 oz/⅓ cup) chia seeds

20 g (¾ oz/¼ cup) rolled (traditional/porridge) oats

2 tablespoons raw cacao powder

½ teaspoon finely grated fresh ginger

200 ml (7 fl oz) tinned coconut milk

200 ml (7 fl oz) fresh or unsweetened coconut water or water

honey or stevia, to taste (optional)

**To serve**

julienned apple (skin on)

sunflower kernels

raw cacao nibs

edible flowers

coconut milk

Combine the apple or pear with the chia seeds, oats, cacao powder and ginger in a bowl and mix well. Add the liquids and stir until combined. Cover and refrigerate for at least 1–2 hours or overnight, stirring occasionally, until thickened. If the pudding becomes too thick, thin with a little water, coconut milk or coconut water to the consistency you like.

Taste the pudding and, if necessary, add a drizzle of honey or a drop or two of stevia to adjust the sweetness to your liking.

Serve the chia pudding into bowls and top with the apple, sunflower kernels, cacao nibs, flowers and coconut milk.

**Makes 4**

**Refined-sugar free | Vegan**

Prepare this chia pudding (without the topping) the night before for an almost instant breakfast. The cacao in this recipe adds a bit of decadence, but it's still completely healthy, so enjoy!

Strawberries and rose water add a fresh and fragrant lightness to this chia breakfast bowl. Make this recipe at the height of strawberry season, when the fruit is at its best.

# Strawberry & rose chia pudding bowl

125 g (4½ oz) strawberries, hulled

60 g (2 oz/⅓ cup) chia seeds

20 g (¾ oz/¼ cup) shredded coconut

250 ml (8½ fl oz/1 cup) fresh or unsweetened coconut water (or water)

100 ml (3½ fl oz) tinned coconut milk

1 teaspoon rose water, plus more if required

**To serve**

sliced strawberries

pomegranate seeds

shaved fresh or dried coconut

fresh or dried rose petals

chopped pistachios

Place the strawberries in a mixing bowl and crush with the back of a fork until roughly mashed and very juicy. Add the chia seeds, shredded coconut, coconut water, coconut milk and rose water and stir well. Cover and refrigerate for at least 1–2 hours or overnight, stirring occasionally, until thickened. If the pudding becomes too thick, thin with a little water, coconut milk or coconut water to the consistency you like.

Taste the pudding and, if necessary, add a little more rose water to balance the flavour to your liking.

Serve the chia pudding into bowls and top with the strawberries, pomegranate seeds, coconut, rose petals and pistachios.

**Makes 4**

**Refined-sugar free | Vegan | Gluten free | Grain free**

# Crunchy citrus toasted granola bowl

225 g (8 oz/2½ cups) rolled (traditional/porridge) oats and/or rolled barley

50 g (1¾ oz/1 cup) flaked or shredded coconut

70 g (2½ oz/½ cup) slivered almonds

50 g (1¾ oz/⅓ cup) pepitas (pumpkin seeds)

45 g (1½ oz/¼ cup) linseeds (flax seeds)

40 g (1½ oz/¼ cup) sesame seeds

2 strips each orange, lemon and lime rind, shredded

1 tablespoon mixed spice

115 g (4 oz/⅓ cup) honey

50 g (1¾ oz) butter, melted

70 g (2½ oz/½ cup) dried dates, chopped

75 g (2¾ oz/½ cup) dried apricots, sliced

2 dried figs, thinly sliced

**To serve (optional)**
natural yoghurt, citrus segments, milk or kefir and shredded citrus zest

Preheat the oven to 130°C/265°F (fan-forced). Line two baking trays with non-stick baking paper.

Combine the rolled oats and/or barley with the coconut, almonds, seeds, shredded rind and mixed spice in a large bowl. Add the honey and butter and mix until well combined.

Spread the mixture over the trays, keeping little clumps of mixture together for extra texture. Bake for about 50 minutes, stirring gently after 25 minutes, until just starting to brown.

Remove from the oven and cool on trays (the granola will crisp as it cools). Gently stir in the dried fruit. This recipe makes about 750 g (1 lb 11 oz/8 cups). Store in an airtight container for up to 2–3 weeks.

To serve, place ½ cup granola in each bowl and, if desired, top with yoghurt and citrus segments. Add a splash of milk or kefir and a scattering of citrus zest.

**Makes 16**

**Refined-sugar free | Vegetarian**

*To make **dairy free**, replace the yoghurt and butter with non-dairy alternatives. To make **vegan**, also swap the honey for rice malt syrup, pure maple syrup or a couple of drops of liquid stevia.*

Homemade toasted granola (muesli) is so satisfying to make. I love it as the hero of a simple breakfast bowl topped with a splash of milk or kefir, or served with fruit and a dollop of yoghurt. It also makes a fantastic crunchy topping for a smoothie bowl or chia pudding.

This recipe makes a big batch and it keeps very well for weeks in an airtight container – that's if it lasts that long! I like to sprinkle it over a bowl of homemade yoghurt (page 75) and top with seasonal fruit. I love the way the tahini accentuates the flavour of the sesame seeds.

# Cacao & black tahini granola bowl

240 g (8½ oz/2½ cups) cooked drained quinoa

80 g (2¾ oz/½ cup) pepitas (pumpkin seeds)

75 g (2¾ oz/½ cup) sunflower kernels

45 g (1½ oz/¼ cup) sesame seeds

45 g (1½ oz/¼ cup) linseeds (flax seeds)

60 g (2 oz/½ cup) pecans, roughly chopped

25 g (1 oz/¼ cup) raw cacao powder

½ teaspoon sea salt flakes

115 g (4 oz/⅓ cup) warmed rice malt syrup

2 tablespoons melted virgin coconut oil

2 tablespoons black tahini

2 teaspoons vanilla extract

100 g (3½ oz/2 cups) flaked or shredded coconut

40 g (1½ oz/⅓ cup) goji berries

### To serve (optional)
Homemade yoghurt (page 75) or coconut yoghurt
strawberries

Preheat the oven to 130°C/265°F (fan-forced). Line two baking trays with non-stick baking paper.

Combine the quinoa, seeds, pecans, cacao powder and salt in a large mixing bowl. Add the rice malt syrup, coconut oil, tahini and vanilla extract and mix until well combined. Add the coconut and mix gently so you don't break up the flakes and it retains some of its white colour.

Spread the mixture over the trays, keeping little clumps of mixture together for extra texture. Bake for about 50 minutes, stirring gently after 25 minutes, until dried out and the coconut is starting to lightly brown.

Remove from the oven and cool on trays (the granola will crisp as it cools). Gently stir in the goji berries. This recipe makes about 800 g (1 lb 12 oz/8 cups). Store in an airtight container for up to 2–3 weeks.

To serve, if desired, place a generous dollop of yoghurt into each serving bowl and top with ½ cup granola and strawberries.

**Makes 16**

**Refined-sugar free | Vegetarian | Gluten free**

*To make **dairy free** and **vegan** replace the yoghurt with a non-dairy alternative.*

# Coconut, sesame & matcha cluster bowl

1 egg white

½ teaspoon fine salt

55 g (2 oz/¼ cup) coconut sugar

75 g (2¾ oz/1½ cups) flaked coconut

40 g (1½ oz/¼ cup) white sesame seeds

40 g (1½ oz/¼ cup) black sesame seeds

35 g (1¼ oz/¼ cup) sunflower kernels

2 teaspoons matcha (green tea) powder

**To serve (optional)**

natural or coconut yoghurt

shredded rose petals or other edible flowers

Preheat the oven to 150°C/300°F (fan-forced). Line a baking tray with non-stick baking paper.

Beat the egg white in a bowl with an electric mixer until frothy and starting to thicken. Add the salt and beat until soft peaks form, then gradually beat in the sugar until thick and glossy. Gently fold in the remaining ingredients.

Spread the mixture over the prepared tray, keeping little clusters of mixture together. Bake for 12–15 minutes, gently stirring every 5 minutes or so (being careful not to break up the clusters too much), until the coconut starts to colour and become fragrant. Watch carefully towards the end of cooking time, as the coconut can burn in the blink of an eye.

Remove from the oven and cool on the tray. This recipe makes about 250 g (9 oz/4½ cups). Store in an airtight container for up to 2–3 weeks (if they last that long).

To serve, if desired, place a generous dollop of yoghurt into each serving bowl and top with ⅓ cup of the coconut, sesame and matcha clusters and sprinkle with flowers.

**Makes 14**

**Refined-sugar free | Vegetarian | Dairy free | Gluten free | Grain free**

These crispy morsels are salty–sweet with an edge of bitterness from the matcha powder. They're fantastic just with yoghurt, or use the clusters as the ultimate crunchy topping on your favourite smoothie bowl.

The use of spelt and buckwheat give this oatmeal (porridge) a great texture. Oats and coconut are a fantastic combination and the caramelised pineapple makes for a very special breakfast.

# Spelt & buckwheat bowl with coconut & pineapple

45 g (1½ oz/½ cup) rolled (traditional/porridge) oats

45 g (1½ oz/½ cup) rolled spelt flakes

50 g (1¾ oz/¼ cup) unhulled buckwheat

2 tablespoons shredded coconut

160 ml (5½ fl oz/⅔ cup) drinking coconut milk

pinch of sea salt flakes

## Caramelised pineapple

20 g (¾ oz) butter

2 tablespoons coconut sugar

6 thin slices fresh pineapple, skin removed and halved

## To serve

coconut cream or coconut yoghurt

toasted flaked coconut (see page 8)

drinking coconut milk

Combine the oats, spelt, buckwheat, coconut and coconut milk with 625 ml (21 fl oz/2½ cups) water and a pinch of salt in a heavy-based saucepan. Cook, stirring occasionally, over medium heat for about 5 minutes until the mixture comes to the boil. Reduce the heat to low and simmer for 6–8 minutes, stirring occasionally, until thickened. The spelt and buckwheat will retain a little bit more texture than the oats. If necessary, thin with a little hot water to reach the consistency you like.

Meanwhile, for the caramelised pineapple, heat the butter and coconut sugar in a heavy-based frying pan over medium heat. Cook, stirring until the sugar is dissolved. Add the pineapple and cook, turning occasionally, for 3–4 minutes or until lightly caramelised.

Serve the oatmeal (porridge) into bowls and top with the caramelised pineapple, coconut cream and coconut. Drizzle with a little of the syrup from the pineapple and add a splash of coconut milk.

**Makes 4**

**Refined-sugar free | Vegetarian**

*To make **dairy free** and **vegan**, use coconut oil instead of butter.*

# Rice-cooker oatmeal with roasted stone fruit

120 g (4½ oz/1⅓ cups) rolled (traditional/porridge) oats
160 ml (5½ fl oz/⅔ cup) milk
sea salt flakes

**Rosemary-roasted stone fruit**

3–4 peaches, nectarines or plums (or a combination)
large handful cherries, pitted
30 g (¾ oz) butter, softened
1–2 tablespoons pure maple syrup
2 sprigs rosemary

**To serve**

pepitas (pumpkin seeds)
sunflower kernels
sprigs of rosemary
natural yoghurt or milk (optional)

To make the rosemary-roasted stone fruit, preheat the oven to 180°C/350°F (fan-forced). Line a roasting pan with non-stick baking paper. Halve or quarter the stone fruit, depending on size, and remove the stones. Place in the prepared pan along with the cherries. Dot the butter over the fruit, drizzle with the maple syrup, adding more if the fruit is a little tart and add 1 tablespoon water to the pan. Add the rosemary and roast for 15–20 minutes, basting the fruit after 10 minutes, or until the fruit is tender and there are some luscious juices in the base of the pan.

Meanwhile, combine the oats and milk with 435 ml (15 fl oz/1¾ cups) water and a pinch of salt in the rice cooker insert. Cover with the lid and turn the rice cooker to the 'oatmeal' or 'porridge' setting if applicable, if not just press 'cook'. The cooker will tell you when the oatmeal is ready (it will switch to 'keep warm'). It should take about 10 minutes. Allow to sit for 2–3 minutes and then give it a good stir. If necessary, thin with a little hot water or milk to reach the consistency you like.

Serve the oatmeal into bowls and top with the roasted fruit, pepitas, sunflower kernels and rosemary. If you like, add yoghurt or a splash of milk.

**Makes 4**

**Refined-sugar free | Vegetarian**

*To make **dairy free** and **vegan**, replace the milk and yoghurt with non-dairy alternatives and swap the butter for coconut oil.*

This is a fantastic way to make oatmeal (porridge) and a good way to get extra mileage out of your rice cooker. You'll need a cooker with a minimum 10-cup capacity. It may take a bit of trial and error with your cooker to get the proportions of oats to water just right.

This 'oatmeal' has a great creamy consistency and the quinoa flakes have an earthiness that pairs beautifully with blueberries and cinnamon. The just-ripe pear adds a little sweetness as well as great texture contrast.

# Quinoa flake & blueberry 'oatmeal'

1 litre (34 fl oz/4 cups)
  milk or water (or a
  combination), plus more
  if required
120 g (4½ oz/1⅓ cups)
  quinoa flakes
65 g (2¼ oz) fresh or frozen
  blueberries
pinch of ground cinnamon
1 firm pear (skin on), grated

**To serve**
thinly sliced firm pear
  (skin on)
fresh, dried and/or
  freeze-dried blueberries
inca berries
milk or milk kefir (optional)
ground cinnamon

Bring the milk or water to the boil in a heavy-based saucepan over medium heat. Stir in the quinoa flakes, blueberries, cinnamon and grated pear. Reduce the heat to medium–low and cook, stirring, for 2–3 minutes, or until thick and creamy. Crush the blueberries lightly against the side of the pan as you stir so they release their juices. If necessary, thin with a little more water or milk to reach the consistency you like.

Serve the oatmeal immediately into bowls and top with pear, blueberries and inca berries. If you like, add a splash of milk or kefir and a sprinkle of cinnamon.

**Makes 4**

**Refined-sugar free | Vegetarian | Gluten free**

*To make **dairy free** and **vegan**, replace the milk and yoghurt with non-dairy alternatives.*

# Coconut amaranth & millet bowl with warm berries

100 g (3½ oz/½ cup) amaranth

100 g (3½ oz/½ cup) hulled millet, rinsed and drained

1½ teaspoons ground cinnamon

1 teaspoon ground ginger

a pinch of sea salt flakes

400 ml (13½ fl oz) tin coconut milk

### Warm mixed berries

225 g (8 oz/1½ cups) frozen mixed berries

1 tablespoon rice malt syrup

shredded zest of 1 orange

### To serve

toasted flaked coconut (see page 8)

coconut milk or coconut yoghurt (optional)

Stir the amaranth in a frying pan over medium heat for about 3 minutes or until fragrant.

Combine the toasted amaranth with the millet, cinnamon, ginger and salt with 500 ml (17 fl oz/2 cups) water in a large saucepan over medium–high heat and bring to the boil. Reduce the heat to low, cover and simmer, stirring occasionally, for 20 minutes or until the water is absorbed. Add the coconut milk, stir well, then cover and simmer, stirring occasionally, for a further 10–15 minutes or until thick and creamy and the grains are tender. The amaranth will still have a nice bit of texture and bite to it.

Meanwhile for the warm mixed berries, combine the berries, rice malt syrup and orange zest in a small saucepan over medium heat. Bring to the boil, stirring occasionally. Reduce the heat to low and simmer for 2–3 minutes or until the berries just begin to break down.

Serve the amaranth mixture into bowls and top with the warm berries and toasted coconut. If you like, add a drizzle of coconut milk or a dollop of coconut yoghurt.

**Makes 4**

**Refined-sugar free | Vegan | Gluten free**

Amaranth is a highly nutritious pseudo-grain with a history reaching back to the Aztecs some 5000 years ago. Toasting amaranth before cooking mellows out the flavour. It blends well with milder-tasting millet and creamy coconut, and retains a pleasing, almost crunchy, popping texture when cooked.

Quinoa and millet complement and balance each other in this recipe. Toasting the seeds for the sprinkle gives them an extra crunchy texture – the sprinkle is a great staple for scattering on just about any breakfast.

# Quinoa & amaranth bowl with toasted sprinkle

200 g (7 oz/1 cup) quinoa, rinsed and drained

55 g (2 oz/¼ cup) amaranth

1 teaspoon natural vanilla extract

½ teaspoon ground cardamom

pinch of sea salt flakes

250 ml (8½ fl oz/1 cup) milk

**Toasted seed sprinkle**

50 g (1¾ oz/⅓ cup) pepitas (pumpkin seeds)

35 g (1¼ oz/¼ cup) sunflower kernels

2 tablespoons sesame seeds

1 tablespoon linseeds (flax seeds)

1 tablespoon coconut sugar

**To serve**

citrus (orange, pink grapefruit and mandarin) slices and/or segments (see page 8)

natural yoghurt or milk (or both)

honey (optional)

To make the toasted seed sprinkle, preheat the oven to 180°C/350°F (fan-forced). Line a baking tray with non-stick baking paper. Combine all of the ingredients in a bowl and then spread the mixture over the prepared tray. Bake for 5–10 minutes or until golden and fragrant. Set aside to cool. Store in an airtight container for up to 2 weeks.

Meanwhile, combine the quinoa, amaranth, vanilla extract, cardamom and salt with 625 ml (21 fl oz/2½ cups) water in a large saucepan over medium–high heat and bring to the boil. Reduce the heat to low, cover and simmer, stirring occasionally, for 20 minutes or until the water is absorbed. Add the milk, stir well, then cover and simmer, stirring occasionally, for a further 5–10 minutes or until thick and somewhat creamy, and the grains are tender.

Serve the quinoa mixture into bowls and top with the fruit, yoghurt or milk and a little toasted seed sprinkle. If you like, drizzle with honey.

**Makes 4**

**Refined-sugar free | Vegetarian | Gluten free**

*To make **dairy free**, replace the yoghurt and/or milk with a non-dairy alternative. To make **vegan**, also swap the honey for rice malt syrup, pure maple syrup or a couple of drops of liquid stevia.*

# Semolina breakfast bowl with poached quinces

15 g (½ oz) butter

130 g (4½ oz/⅔ cup) semolina

500 ml (17 fl oz/2 cups) milk

2 tablespoons rice malt syrup

1 teaspoon ground cardamom

½ vanilla bean, split and seeds scraped

**Spiced poached quinces**

zest and juice 1 orange

115 g (4 oz/⅓ cup) rice malt syrup

1 tablespoon lemon juice

1 cinnamon stick

½ vanilla bean, split and seeds scraped

4 cardamom pods, bruised

8 black peppercorns

2 quinces

**To serve**

natural yoghurt

roughly chopped pistachios

ground cardamom

milk (optional)

To make the quinces, place all the ingredients except the quinces in a large heavy-based saucepan with 500 ml (17 fl oz/2 cups) water. Bring slowly to the boil over medium–low heat, stirring occasionally to dissolve the syrup. Meanwhile, peel the quinces one at a time (reserve the peel) and cut each into 6 or 8 wedges, leaving the core intact. Add the quince to the syrup in the pan. Tie the peel in a piece of muslin to enclose then add to the pan. Reduce the heat to a simmer, partially cover with the lid and cook for 1½–2 hours or until the quinces are a deep pink–red colour and are soft, but still holding their form. Cool the quinces in the liquid or serve warm. The cores of the quinces may be removed before serving. Discard the muslin bag, vanilla bean pod and spices. Store, covered, in the refrigerator for up to 4 days.

Melt the butter in a heavy-based saucepan over medium heat. Add the semolina and cook, stirring, for 4–5 minutes or until light golden and fragrant. Transfer to a bowl.

Add the milk, rice malt syrup, cardamom, and vanilla seeds and pod to the pan with 500 ml (17 fl oz/2 cups) water. Bring to the boil over medium–high heat. Add the semolina and return to the boil, stirring constantly. Cook, uncovered, stirring, for 2–3 minutes or until mixture thickens. If necessary, thin with a little hot water or milk. Remove from the heat and discard the vanilla bean pod.

Serve the semolina into bowls and top with yoghurt, the poached quince and a drizzle of the poaching syrup. Sprinkle with pistachios and cardamom and, if you like, add a splash of milk.

**Makes 4**

**Refined-sugar free | Vegetarian**

*To make **vegan**, replace the butter with coconut oil, and the milk and yoghurt with non-dairy alternatives.*

Toasting the semolina before cooking is not necessary for this recipe to be successful; however, it does give the dish a pleasing mellow nuttiness, adding an extra dimension to the flavour. The quinces will take a couple of hours to cook, but they can be prepared a few days ahead of time.

Bircher muesli (overnight oats) is not only creamy, textural and delicious, it's also a convenient breakfast because it is best made the night before. Soaking the grains and seeds makes it easier for your body to absorb the nutrients. I like to mix it up with grains, but by all means just use oats if that's what you have in your pantry.

# Mixed-grain bircher muesli

90 g (3 oz/1 cup) rolled
(traditional/porridge)
oats

60 g (2 oz/¼ cup) raw
unhulled buckwheat,
rinsed

30 g (1 oz/⅓ cup) rolled
spelt flakes

30 g (1 oz/⅓ cup) rolled
barley flakes

1 tablespoon linseeds
(flax seeds)

1 teaspoon ground
cinnamon

juice and pulp of 2 large
oranges

1 nashi or pear (skin on),
grated

250 g (9 oz/1 cup) Greek-
style yoghurt or 250 ml
(8½ fl oz/1 cup) milk kefir

**To serve**

quartered fresh figs

fresh berries

chopped roasted almonds

tahini

sesame seeds

milk or milk kefir (optional)

Combine the oats, buckwheat, spelt, barley, linseeds, cinnamon
and orange juice and pulp in a medium-sized bowl. Add about
180 ml (6 fl oz/¾ cup) water, or just enough to ensure the mixture is
just covered in liquid. Cover and refrigerate for at least 2 hours, or,
ideally, overnight.

Just before serving, stir in the grated nashi or pear and the yoghurt or
kefir. Serve the bircher into bowls and top with the fruit and almonds.
Drizzle with tahini, scatter with sesame seeds and, if you like, add a
splash of milk or kefir.

**Makes 4**

**Refined-sugar free | Vegetarian**

*To make **vegan**, replace the yoghurt or milk kefir with a non-dairy
alternative.*

# Gluten-free bircher muesli

25 g (1 oz/½ cup) coconut flakes

50 g (1¾ oz/¼ cup) raw unhulled buckwheat, rinsed

20 g (¾ oz/¼ cup) quinoa flakes

35 g (1¼ oz/¼ cup) pepitas (pumpkin seeds)

35 g (1¼ oz/¼ cup) sunflower kernels

1 tablespoon linseeds (flax seeds)

1 tablespoon roasted black sesame seeds

1 tablespoon goji berries

juice and pulp of 1 orange

1 nashi or pear (skin on), cut into matchsticks

125 g (4½ oz/½ cup) coconut yoghurt

**To serve**
shredded apple or pear, cherries, inca berries, hemp seeds, rice malt syrup (optional), coconut milk (optional)

Combine the coconut flakes, buckwheat, quinoa flakes, pepitas, sunflower kernels, linseeds, sesame seeds, goji berries and orange juice and pulp in a medium-sized bowl. Add about 125 ml (4 fl oz/½ cup) water, or just enough to ensure the mixture is just covered in liquid. Cover and refrigerate for at least 2 hours, or, ideally, overnight.

Just before serving, stir in the nashi or pear and the yoghurt. Serve the bircher into bowls and top with fruit and seeds. If you like, drizzle with rice malt syrup and add a splash of coconut milk.

**Makes 4**

**Refined-sugar free | Vegan | Gluten free**

This bircher muesli (overnight oats) is full of amazing texture. Each seed adds its own unique character. Soaking the grains makes the nutrients more readily available for your body to absorb. If you don't need this recipe to be vegan or dairy free, natural yoghurt is a great alternative for the coconut yoghurt and you can use honey in place of the rice malt syrup.

This recipe borrows a bit from several Asian cuisines. It is not faithful to any one country, but is delightful all the same. If you don't have a chance to soak the rice overnight, it will take about 15–20 minutes longer to cook and you'll need to add a little more water as the rice starts to thicken.

# Black rice breakfast bowl with tropical fruit

400 ml (13½ fl oz) tin coconut milk, chilled overnight

200 g (7 oz/1 cup) glutinous (sticky) black rice, soaked overnight in cold water and drained

2 strips pandan leaf, tied in a knot or ½ teaspoon pandan essence

2 tablespoons coconut sugar or rapadura sugar

pinch of sea salt flakes

**To serve**

sliced mango

lychees

toasted flaked coconut (see page 8)

shredded lime zest

crushed toasted sesame seeds (see page 8)

Carefully open the tin of coconut milk and scoop out 80 ml (2½ fl oz/⅓ cup) of the thickened coconut cream from the top of the tin. Place in a small bowl, cover and refrigerate until needed.

Place the drained rice in a large heavy-based saucepan. Add the remaining coconut milk from the tin, along with the pandan leaf or essence and 375 ml (12½ fl oz/1½ cups) water. Bring to the boil over medium–high heat, stirring occasionally. Reduce the heat to low and simmer, stirring occasionally for 30–35 minutes or until the rice is tender. Keep a close eye on the mixture as it starts to thicken. Add a little more hot water if the rice becomes too dry and starts to stick to the pan.

When the rice is tender, stir in the sugar and a pinch of salt. Cook for 2–3 minutes or until it reaches the consistency you like (I like it so that it falls from the spoon in heavy dollops). Remove and discard the pandan leaves.

Serve the rice into bowls and top with the reserved coconut cream along with mango, lychees, toasted coconut, lime zest and a sprinkle of sesame seeds.

**Makes 4**

**Refined-sugar free | Vegan | Gluten free**

# Classic bowls

Making your own yoghurt is very simple and economical. The main resource required is time – you just need to think ahead. I like to prepare the mixture early in the morning (before work), allow it to rest and culture during the day, then place it in the refrigerator to chill overnight, ready for the next day.

# Homemade natural yoghurt bowl

2 litres (68 fl oz/8 cups) full cream milk

160 g (5½ oz/⅔ cup) plain (natural or Greek-style) unsweetened yoghurt with live cultures

**To serve (optional)**
passionfruit pulp
edible flowers

Pour the milk into a large heavy-based saucepan over medium heat and heat the milk to 85°C (185°F), whisking often to ensure even heating and prevent scorching on the base of the pan.

Remove from the heat and allow to cool to 45°C (113°F), whisking occasionally. To bring the temperature down, half-fill your kitchen sink with cold water and stand the pot in the sink. When the milk reaches 45°C (113°F), transfer 250 ml (8½ fl oz/1 cup) to a mixing bowl. Add the yoghurt (this is your 'starter') and whisk well until combined. Return this mixture to the milk in the saucepan and whisk gently until combined.

Pour into two 1 litre (34 fl oz/4 cup) sterilised jars. Cover loosely (but do not seal), wrap each jar with a clean kitchen towel and then in clean bath towels to maintain the temperature for as long as possible. Place in a safe, preferably warm, place and leave for 6–8 hours, until thickened and soured to your liking. Seal the jars and refrigerate for 3–4 hours until well chilled. Use within 7 days.

If you like, serve with passionfruit pulp and edible flowers, or use wherever natural yoghurt is called for in any of the recipes in this book.

- *The longer you leave the yoghurt to culture and set, the more sour it will become (to a certain point, when all the milk sugars are converted to lactic acid). It can take a bit of trial and error to get the flavour just as you like it.*

- *For thicker yoghurt, add a couple of tablespoons of skim (or whole) milk powder to the milk when you heat it.*

- *You can reuse your homemade yoghurt as the starter 3–4 times before it will get 'tired' and the flavour will change.*

- *To make labneh see page 79 for the method.*

**Makes about 2 kg (4 lb 6 oz/8 cups)**

**Refined-sugar free | Vegetarian | Gluten free | Grain free**

# Choc–avocado mousse with berries & granola

60 g (2 oz) fresh (medjool) dates, seeded and roughly chopped

3 bananas

1 avocado, stone removed

35 g (1¼ oz/⅓ cup) raw cacao powder

**To serve**

Crunchy citrus toasted granola (page 48)

fresh berries

edible flowers

Put the dates in a small heatproof bowl and cover with warm water. Leave to soak for 10 minutes. Drain, discarding the water, and transfer the dates to a food processor with the banana, avocado and cacao powder. Whiz until smooth.

Serve the mousse into bowls and top with the granola, berries and flowers.

**Makes 4**

**Refined-sugar free | Vegan**

While this may feel like you're eating dessert for breakfast, this mousse is a fantastically healthy start to the day.

You will need to start this recipe the day before, as the yoghurt needs to strain overnight. Use your delicious homemade yoghurt (page 75) for this recipe, or your favourite natural or Greek-style yoghurt. If you do use store-bought, pot-set yoghurt will work best.

# Vanilla labneh bowl with sweet dukkah

macadamia oil, for rolling

2 oranges, peeled and sliced

½ small watermelon, cut into wedges

orange blossom water, to taste

5 fresh (medjool) dates, sliced lengthways

pistachios, to serve

edible flowers, to serve

### Labneh

600 g (1 lb 5 oz) Homemade yoghurt (page 75) or natural or Greek-style yoghurt

½ teaspoon vanilla bean paste (omit for savoury recipes using this labneh)

### Sweet vanilla dukkah

40 g (1½ oz) sesame seeds

2 tablespoons pistachios

2 tablespoons toasted hazelnuts (see page 8)

2 teaspoons coconut sugar

1 teaspoon vanilla bean powder or ½ teaspoon vanilla bean paste

¼ teaspoon ground cinnamon

pinch of sea salt flakes

To make the labneh, line a sieve with a double thickness of clean muslin (cheesecloth) and place over a bowl. Place the yoghurt in the lined sieve then bring the cloth up and around the yoghurt to enclose it. Twist the cloth at the top or tie with string. Cover with plastic wrap and place in the refrigerator to strain for at least 6–8 hours or overnight (the longer you strain it for, the thicker it will become – you'll lose about 50% of the volume if you strain overnight). Tip the labneh from the strainer into a bowl and stir in the vanilla bean paste. Reserve the whey left over in the straining bowl for another use; it's great in smoothie bowls and salad dressings, or your pets will love it for a treat. This recipe makes about 250 g (9 oz/1 cup). Store in an airtight container in the fridge for up to 4 days.

To make the dukkah, toast the sesame seeds in a dry frying pan for 3–4 minutes or until fragrant. Lightly crush using a mortar and pestle, then add the pistachios and hazelnuts and pound until the nuts are just broken down (make sure you retain some texture). Stir in the remaining ingredients. This recipe makes about 100 g (3½ oz/⅔ cup). Store in an airtight container for up to 2 weeks.

Oil your hands very lightly with the oil and roll tablespoonfuls of the labneh into balls. Roll gently in the dukkah to coat entirely. Set aside.

Arrange the orange and watermelon in wide shallow bowls and sprinkle with a little orange blossom water. Top with the labneh and scatter with the dates, pistachios and flowers.

**Makes 4**

**Refined-sugar free | Vegetarian | Gluten free | Grain free**

# Seasonal fruit & yoghurt bowl

500 g (1 lb 2 oz/2 cups) Homemade yoghurt (page 75)

**To serve**
fresh fruit, such as apple, stone fruit, kiwi fruit, watermelon, berries and dragon fruit
Crunchy citrus toasted granola (page 48)
goji berries or other dried fruit
bee pollen
edible flowers
honey (optional)

Serve the yoghurt into bowls and top with the fruit, granola, goji berries or other dried fruit, bee pollen and edible flowers.

If you like, drizzle with a little honey.

**Makes 4**

**Refined-sugar free | Vegetarian | Gluten free**

It is hard to beat the luscious simplicity of this beautiful bowl. Swirls of your favourite creamy yoghurt topped with the sweetest in-season fruit and a scattering of homemade granola for crunch. If you use your own homemade yoghurt and it is not quite thick enough, it will benefit from an hour or so draining in a piece of muslin (cheesecloth) lining a sieve.

Add a hit of caffeine to your morning oats, bringing two of the best things about breakfast together in one bowl. The lemon juice in the coffee syrup adds an extra, exceptional dimension to the flavour.

# Morning coffee oatmeal

120 g (4½ oz/1⅓ cups) rolled (traditional/porridge) oats

2 tablespoons sultanas (golden raisins) or sliced dried dates (optional)

160 ml (5½ fl oz/⅔ cup) milk

pinch of sea salt flakes

### Coffee syrup

1 tablespoon rapadura or dark brown sugar

1 teaspoon Dutch-processed cacao powder

60 ml (2 fl oz/¼ cup) freshly brewed espresso or good-quality strong instant coffee

lemon juice, to taste

### To serve

natural or Greek-style yoghurt

sliced fresh (medjool) dates

raw cacao nibs

Combine the oats, sultanas or dates (if using) and milk with 625ml (21 fl oz/2½ cups) water and a pinch of salt in a heavy-based saucepan. Cook over medium heat for about 5 minutes, stirring occasionally, until the mixture comes to the boil. Reduce the heat to low and simmer for 5–6 minutes, stirring occasionally, until thickened. Add a little more milk or hot water to adjust the consistency.

Meanwhile, for the coffee syrup, stir the sugar, cacao powder, a tiny pinch of salt and coffee until dissolved. Add lemon juice a little at a time, to taste.

Serve the oatmeal (porridge) into bowls, swirl the yoghurt through and drizzle with the coffee syrup. Scatter with the sliced dates and cacao nibs.

**Makes 4**

**Refined-sugar free | Vegetarian**

# Caramelised apple & blueberry crumble bowl

20 g (¾ oz) butter

1 tablespoon honey

3 granny smith (or other cooking) apples (skin on), cut into thin wedges

225 g (8 oz/1½ cups) frozen or fresh blueberries

2 teaspoons vanilla bean paste

finely grated zest and juice of 1 orange

natural or coconut yoghurt, to serve

edible flowers, to serve

## Crumble

40 g (1½ oz) butter, melted

2 tablespoons tahini

45 g (1½ oz/½ cup) quinoa flakes

25 g (1 oz/½ cup) coconut flakes

10 g (¼ oz/1 cup) puffed buckwheat cereal

2 tablespoons coconut sugar

2 tablespoons sesame seeds

1 teaspoon ground cinnamon

Preheat the oven to 160°C/320°F (fan-forced).

Heat the butter and honey in a large heavy-based frying pan over medium heat. Add the apple and cook, stirring occasionally, for 5–10 minutes or until the apples are starting to colour and soften. Remove the pan from the heat and stir in the blueberries, vanilla bean paste and the orange zest and juice. Spoon into four ovenproof bowls.

For the crumble topping, whisk the butter and tahini together in a large bowl. Add the remaining ingredients and stir until the dry ingredients are well coated.

Sprinkle the crumble mixture over the fruit. Bake for 30–35 minutes or until the fruit is bubbling and the top is golden and crisp. Cover with foil if the top is browning too quickly. Serve with a dollop of yoghurt and scatter with flowers.

**Makes 4**

**Refined-sugar free | Vegetarian | Gluten free**

*To make **dairy free**, replace the butter with coconut oil. To make **vegan**, also swap the honey for rice malt syrup, pure maple syrup or a couple of drops of liquid stevia.*

This crumble topping has so much interesting texture and a great nutty flavour.

These creamy steel-cut oats are ready in 25–30 minutes and reheat beautifully for the rest of the week if you have any leftovers. If you want to give the oats an extra dimension and real depth of flavour, toast them in a frying pan with a small knob of butter for 2–3 minutes until they just start to crackle and become fragrant. Do this as you heat the milk and water.

# Steel-cut oats with poached rhubarb & strawberries

250 ml (8½ fl oz/1 cup) milk, plus extra to serve (optional)

180 g (6½ oz/1 cup) steel-cut oats

pinch of sea salt flakes

### Caramelised macadamia sprinkle

35 g (1¼ oz/¼ cup) roughly chopped macadamia nuts

1 tablespoon sunflower kernels

2 tablespoons pure maple syrup

½ teaspoon ground cinnamon

### Poached rhubarb and strawberries

300 g (10½ oz/about ½ bunch) rhubarb, cut into 3 cm (1¼ in) pieces

250 g (9 oz) strawberries, hulled and halved if large

zest and juice of 1 orange

pure maple syrup or honey, to taste

Combine the milk with 750 ml (25½ fl oz/3 cups) water in a large heavy-based saucepan over medium heat. Bring to the boil and stir in the oats and salt. Reduce the heat to medium–low and simmer gently for 20–25 minutes, stirring occasionally, until the mixture is thick and creamy. As the mixture starts to thicken and catch on the bottom of the pan, reduce the heat to low. If necessary, thin with a little hot water or milk to reach the consistency you like.

Meanwhile, to make the caramelised macadamia sprinkle, heat the macadamia nuts, sunflower kernels, maple syrup and cinnamon in a small frying pan over medium heat. Cook, shaking the pan constantly for 2–3 minutes or until the mixture has thickened slightly and is sticky. Spoon onto a baking paper-lined baking tray and set aside to cool. Break into pieces.

To make the poached rhubarb and strawberries, combine the rhubarb, strawberries, orange zest and juice in a small saucepan over medium heat. Bring to the boil, reduce the heat to medium–low and simmer, covered, for 2–3 minutes or until the fruit is just tender. Taste and add a little maple syrup or honey if the mixture is too tart. May be served warm or cold. The poached fruit will keep for a few days in a sealed container in the fridge or portion it into serving sizes in small zip-lock bags and freeze for up to 6 weeks.

Serve the oats into bowls and top with the poached fruit and macadamia sprinkle. If you like, add a splash of extra milk.

**Makes 4**

**Refined-sugar free | Vegetarian**

*To make **vegan**, replace the milk with a non-dairy alternative and use maple syrup in the poached fruit, if necessary.*

# Rhubarb & pear crumble bowl

300 g (10½ oz) rhubarb, cut into pieces

2 pears (skin on), peeled and cut into pieces

2 teaspoons vanilla bean paste

1 tablespoon honey, plus extra to serve (optional)

zest and juice of 1 orange

natural or coconut yoghurt, to serve

pepitas (pumpkin seeds), to serve

toasted flaked coconut (see page 8), to serve

## Crumble

100 g (3½ oz/1 cup) rolled (traditional/porridge) oats

50 g (1¾ oz/⅓ cup) plain (all-purpose) flour

2 tablespoons sunflower kernels

1 tablespoon linseeds (flax seeds)

2 teaspoons mixed spice

80 g (2¾ oz) butter, chopped

2 tablespoons honey

Preheat the oven to 160°C/320°F (fan-forced).

Combine the rhubarb, pear, vanilla bean paste, honey, orange zest and juice in a large bowl. Spoon into four ovenproof bowls.

For the crumble topping, combine the oats, flour, sunflower kernels, linseeds and mixed spice in a large bowl. Add the butter and honey. Use your fingertips to rub in the butter until well combined, but still clumpy.

Sprinkle the crumble mixture over the fruit, leaving little clumps of different sizes. Bake for 35–40 minutes or until the fruit is tender and bubbling, and the top is golden and crisp. Cover with foil if the top is browning too quickly. Serve warm with a dollop of yoghurt, pepitas and a drizzle of honey.

**Makes 4**

**Refined-sugar free | Vegetarian**

*To make **dairy free**, replace the butter with coconut oil. To make **vegan**, also swap the honey for rice malt syrup, pure maple syrup or a couple of drops of liquid stevia.*

If your pears are not quite ripe, they will benefit from a little pre-cooking. Place the chopped pears in a medium-sized saucepan with a splash of water and simmer over medium heat, covered, for 5 or so minutes until just starting to become tender.

This creamy rice bowl is incredibly luxurious and fragrant. It is delicious served warm and silky, or the next day when it has thickened slightly.

# Creamy Middle Eastern rice bowl

150 g (5½ oz/¾ cup)
  medium-grain rice
1 cinnamon stick
pinch of salt
750 ml (25½ fl oz/3 cups)
  milk
1½ tablespoons honey
1 vanilla bean, split with
  seeds scraped
finely grated zest of
  1 lemon

**To serve**
roughly chopped pistachios
pomegranate seeds
pomegranate molasses
dried rose petals

Combine the rice, cinnamon stick and a pinch of salt with 310 ml (10½ fl oz/1¼ cups) water in a heavy-based saucepan and bring to the boil over high heat. Cover with a tight-fitting lid and reduce the heat to very low. Cook for 10 minutes or until the water is absorbed.

Stir the milk, honey and vanilla seeds and pod into the rice and bring to the boil over medium heat. Reduce the heat to medium–low and simmer, uncovered and stirring often for 15–20 minutes, until the rice is tender and the mixture is thick and creamy. Stir in the lemon zest. Set aside to cool slightly and remove and discard the cinnamon stick and vanilla pod.

Serve the creamy rice warm or cool, topped with the pistachios and pomegranate seeds, a drizzle of pomegranate molasses and sprinkled with rose petals.

**Makes 4**

**Refined-sugar free | Gluten free**

*To make **dairy free**, swap the milk for a non-dairy alternative. To make **vegan**, also swap the honey for rice malt syrup, pure maple syrup or a couple of drops of liquid stevia.*

# Orange blossom bread & butter pudding

50 g (1¾ oz) fresh (medjool) dates, seeded and sliced

2 tablespoons roughly chopped almonds

2 tablespoons sliced dried apricots

finely grated zest of 1 orange

1 tablespoon orange blossom water

30 g (1 oz) butter, softened (optional)

4 x 2 cm (¾ in) thick slices sourdough rye bread

4 free-range eggs

625 ml (21 fl oz/2½ cups) milk

**To serve**
yoghurt
ground cinnamon
honey (optional)

Preheat the oven to 140°C/275°F (fan-forced). Place four shallow ovenproof bowls onto a baking tray.

Combine the dates, almonds, apricots, orange zest and 2 teaspoons of the orange blossom water in a bowl and set aside.

Butter the bread if you like and cut into cubes, leaving the crust on, and pile into the bowls. Sprinkle with the fruit mixture, tucking it between the bread cubes.

Whisk the eggs, milk and remaining orange blossom water together in a large jug. Pour evenly over the bread and fruit and set aside to rest for 10 minutes, allowing some of the liquid to absorb into the bread.

Bake for 40–45 minutes or until puffed in the centre, golden and set.

To serve, top with yoghurt, a sprinkle of cinnamon and, if you like, a drizzle of honey.

**Makes 4**

**Refined-sugar free | Vegetarian**

*To make **dairy free**, leave out the butter and swap the milk and yoghurt for non-dairy alternatives.*

This healthy take on a comforting dessert makes for a perfect breakfast. You can leave out the butter if you like, and a drizzle of honey for extra sweetness is optional. I do like to keep the crusts on my bread as it adds a nice chewy texture.

I love this hands-off method of cooking oats. If peaches are out of season, try apple or pear instead. The blueberries provide a great 'pop' of sweetness when you bite into them, but any berry will do. The whipped ricotta is lovely, but if you're after an instant topping, a good dollop of yoghurt is great too.

# Baked oatmeal with lemon thyme & ricotta

3 peaches, sliced

2 teaspoons fresh lemon thyme leaves, plus extra to serve

135 g (5 oz/1½ cups) rolled (traditional/porridge) oats

250 ml (8½ fl oz/1 cup) milk

125 g (4½ oz) frozen or fresh blueberries

25 g (1 oz/¼ cup) roughly chopped walnuts

2 tablespoons sunflower kernels

1 tablespoon linseeds (flax seeds)

sliced plum, to serve

pure maple syrup, to serve (optional)

## Whipped ricotta

240 g (8½ oz/1 cup) firm fresh ricotta

1 tablespoon pure maple syrup

1 teaspoon vanilla bean paste

Preheat the oven to 160°C/320°F (fan-forced). Place four small ovenproof bowls onto a baking tray.

Divide two-thirds of the peach slices over the bases of the bowls and sprinkle with the lemon thyme and oats. Combine the milk with 500 ml (17 fl oz/2 cups) water in a jug and pour gently and evenly over the oats in each bowl. Make sure the oats are spread evenly in the bowls.

Bake for 15 minutes, then remove from the oven and give the mixture a light stir with a fork, pressing the oats under the liquid slightly, if necessary. Sprinkle with the blueberries, walnuts, sunflower kernels and linseeds and return to the oven for a further 10–12 minutes or until the oats are tender and there is very little liquid left. Remove from the oven and set aside for 5 minutes.

Meanwhile, for the whipped ricotta, whiz the ricotta, maple syrup and vanilla bean paste in a food processor or blender until smooth. If necessary, thin with a little water or milk to reach the consistency you like. Transfer to a small bowl, cover and refrigerate until required.

Serve the oatmeal warm, topped with the whipped ricotta, sliced plum, remaining peach slices and extra thyme. If you like, drizzle with maple syrup.

**Makes 4**

**Refined-sugar free | Vegetarian**

*To make **vegan**, swap the milk for a non-dairy alternative and replace the whipped ricotta with coconut yoghurt.*

# Banana-split bowl with bircher muesli

4 bananas, halved
  lengthways
½ quantity Mixed-grain
  bircher muesli (page 67)
250 g (9 oz/1 cup) labneh
  (see page 79) or yoghurt

**To serve**
balled cantaloupe and
  watermelon (see page 8)
edible flowers
bee pollen
milk (optional)

Serve the banana into four shallow bowls. Top the banana with the bircher muesli, labneh or yoghurt, melon balls, flowers and bee pollen. If you like, add a splash of milk.

**Makes 4**

**Refined-sugar free | Vegetarian**

*To make **dairy free**, make the vegan variation of the mixed-grain bircher muesli, and swap the labneh and milk for non-dairy alternatives. To make **vegan**, also leave out the bee pollen.*

These banana splits are delightfully luxurious served with labneh – almost like eating dessert for breakfast. If you don't have time to make labneh, creamy natural yoghurt is almost as good.

# Comfort bowls

Congee is such a comforting breakfast. It is easy to see why it is so popular, with slight variations, all over Asia. Vary the topping depending on your mood. I've used some of my favourite ingredients here, but you could try soy, chilli or fish sauce, fried shallots or garlic, roasted crushed peanuts, pickled vegetables or kimchi.

# Chicken congee

200 g (7 oz/1 cup) long grain white rice
2 skinless chicken thigh cutlets, trimmed
5 cm (2 in) piece fresh ginger, sliced
handful coriander (cilantro) sprigs
1 litre (34 fl oz/4 cups) homemade or good quality chicken stock

**To serve**
coriander (cilantro) leaves
shredded spring onion (scallions)
thinly sliced fresh chilli
roasted black sesame seeds
sesame oil
other condiments such as fried shallots or garlic, crushed peanuts, pickled vegetables and/or kimchi (optional)

Combine the rice, chicken, ginger, coriander and stock with 1.5 litres (51 fl oz/6 cups) water and a good pinch each of salt and pepper in a large heavy-based saucepan over medium–high heat. Bring to the boil, stirring often, and then reduce the heat to medium–low and simmer steadily, partially covered, stirring occasionally for 30 minutes. Remove the chicken and set aside to cool slightly. Continue cooking the congee for a further 30 minutes or until the rice has broken down and the mixture is thick and creamy. You may need to reduce the heat slightly as the mixture starts to thicken to avoid sticking to the bottom of the pan.

Meanwhile, when the chicken is cool enough to handle, shred the chicken from the bones. Set the chicken aside and return the bones to the congee to extract any remaining flavour from them.

Remove the cooked congee from the heat and fish out and discard the chicken bones and ginger. Stir the shredded chicken into the congee, taste, and season with a little more salt and pepper if needed.

Ladle into bowls and top with coriander leaves, spring onion, chilli, sesame seeds and sesame oil. If you like, serve any other condiments on the side.

**Makes 4**

**Refined-sugar free | Dairy free | Gluten free**

# Chicken pho

3 red Asian shallots, unpeeled

6 cm (2½ in) piece young ginger

1.5 kg (3 lb 5 oz) whole organic chicken

1.5 kg (3 lb 5 oz) chicken bones or carcasses, washed

3 star anise

1 cinnamon stick

1 teaspoon coriander seeds

1 teaspoon fennel seeds

½ teaspoon black peppercorns

2 tablespoons fish sauce

400 g (14 oz) fresh rice noodles

120 g (4½ oz) bean sprouts

1 carrot, shredded into long strips

**To serve**

fish sauce, fresh herb sprigs (such as mint and coriander/cilantro), finely sliced red chilli, chilli sauce, lime cheeks

Char the shallots and ginger directly over a gas flame on a stovetop or barbecue until blackened all over. Set aside to cool slightly. When cool enough to handle, peel and slice the shallots and ginger.

Meanwhile, joint the chicken, discarding any fat: cut off the wings and legs and cut each into two pieces through the joints. Cut away the back bone and then cut through the breast bone to separate the breasts. Place the chicken bones or carcasses and the jointed chicken pieces, including the backbone, into a large stockpot and add enough cold water to cover the bones (about 3 litres/101 fl oz). Tie the spices in a clean piece of muslin (cheesecloth) and add to the pot along with the shallot and ginger and the fish sauce. Bring the water slowly to a simmer over medium heat, skimming off the impurities that rise to the surface. Reduce the heat to medium–low and simmer gently for about 30 minutes or until the chicken on the breast bones is just cooked through. Remove all the chicken pieces, except the wings, from the pot with a long pair of tongs (leaving the stock to continue simmering) and set aside until cool enough to handle. Strip the meat from the bones, discard the skin and return the bones to the pot. Cover the chicken meat and set aside for later. Continue to simmer the stock gently, skimming the surface occasionally to remove any fat for a further 60–90 minutes until flavoursome. Do not let the stock boil or it may become cloudy. Strain, discarding the solids.

Blanch the noodles in simmering water for 1 minute, carefully separating them. Strain and divide into bowls, top with the shredded chicken, bean sprouts and carrot, and pour over the piping hot stock.

Serve with fish sauce, herbs, sliced chilli, chilli sauce and lime cheeks on the side.

**Makes 4**

**Refined-sugar free | Dairy free | Gluten free**

This pho recipe is not strictly traditional, but it embodies the essence of Vietnam and contains all the flavours I love. The broth is aromatic and slightly spicy and the herbs add a fresh zing. If you're lucky enough to have any broth left over, freeze it and use it another day.

Cooking bacon pieces with a little water helps make it super crispy. I love the way the sriracha splatters like graffiti over the sunny eggs in this bowl. Sweet potato makes a nice alternative to regular potato, plus it has more fibre, vitamins A and C, and is lower in carbohydrates and kilojoules (calories).

# Chilli bacon & eggs with sweet potato hash

200 g (7 oz) thickly
   sliced smoky bacon or
   kaiserfleisch, cut into 1 cm
   (½ in) pieces
½ red onion, cut into thin
   wedges
2 orange sweet potatoes,
   peeled and cut into
   1.5 cm (½ in) pieces
2–3 tablespoons olive oil
4 free-range eggs
1 avocado, stone removed,
   sliced

**To serve**
labneh (see page 79)
fresh coriander (cilantro)
   leaves
finely sliced red or green
   chilli
sriracha or other hot sauce

Combine the bacon with 80 ml (2½ fl oz/⅓ cup) water in a large heavy-based frying pan over medium–high heat. Cook, stirring occasionally until the water evaporates and the fat renders from the bacon. Cook for a few more minutes until the bacon is very crisp. Remove with a slotted spoon and drain on paper towel.

Reduce the heat to medium and add the onion to the pan, cook for 1–2 minutes or until slightly softened, then remove from the pan with a slotted spoon and drain. Add the sweet potato to the pan along with a little olive oil if the pan is becoming dry. Cook for 15–20 minutes, stirring occasionally, but not too often as you want a crust to form on the sweet potato. When the sweet potato is tender and well browned, return the bacon and onion to the pan to heat through.

When the sweet potato is almost done, heat another frying pan over medium heat with a splash of olive oil. Carefully break the eggs into the pan and cook for 2–2½ minutes until the whites are crispy around the edges, but the yolks are still runny (or until cooked to your liking).

Serve the sweet potato hash into bowls and top with the avocado and fried eggs. Add a dollop of labneh, a scattering of coriander and chilli and, if you like, a squeeze of sriracha.

**Makes 4**

**Refined-sugar free | Gluten free | Grain free**

*To make **vegetarian**, leave out the bacon.*

# Ginger & turmeric rice bowl with crispy egg & kimchi

200 g (7 oz/1 cup) basmati rice, rinsed
60 ml (2 fl oz/¼ cup) peanut oil
4 spring onions (scallions), chopped
1 tablespoon sesame seeds
1 teaspoon finely grated fresh ginger
1 garlic clove, very finely sliced
1 teaspoon ground turmeric
4 free-range eggs
1 bunch broccolini, trimmed

**To serve**
kimchi
shredded spring onion
roasted black sesame seeds
sesame oil
tamari or soy sauce

Add the rice to a large saucepan with 375 ml (12½ fl oz/1½ cups) water. Bring to the boil, cover with a tight-fitting lid and reduce the heat to low. Cook for 10 minutes and then turn off the heat. Without lifting the lid, set the saucepan aside for 10 minutes to rest. Spread the rice over a large tray to cool slightly.

Heat 2 tablespoons of the oil in a large heavy-based frying pan (cast iron if you have one) or wok over medium heat. Add the spring onion, sesame seeds, ginger, garlic and half of the turmeric and cook, stirring, for about 1 minute or until fragrant. Add the rice and stir-fry until heated through, about 2 minutes. Season with salt. Increase the heat to medium–high and let the rice cook, undisturbed, for a further 3–4 minutes so that a crunchy crust forms on the bottom. Be careful that it doesn't burn – turn the heat down a little if necessary.

Meanwhile, heat the remaining oil in a separate heavy-based frying pan over medium–high heat. Add the remaining turmeric and swirl the pan to combine. Carefully break the eggs into the pan and cook for 2–2½ minutes until the whites are crispy around the edges, but the yolks are still runny (or until cooked to your liking).

At the same time, in a steamer basket set over a large saucepan of simmering water, steam the broccolini for 2 minutes or until tender but still crisp.

Serve the rice into bowls, ensuring every bowl gets a share of the crispy rice. Top with the broccolini, fried eggs, kimchi, spring onion and sesame seeds. Serve the sesame oil and tamari or soy sauce on the side.

**Makes 4**

**Refined-sugar free | Vegetarian | Dairy free | Gluten free**

The rice can be cooked the day before and stored in an airtight container in the refrigerator (or use leftovers from last night's dinner). Gently break it up with your hands before cooking. The crispy rice makes this breakfast bowl extra delicious – I find my large cast iron frying pan gives me the best result.

This is a bit of a jumble of Southeast Asian flavours that work brilliantly together. I've used laksa paste for instant impact with a few fresh aromatics for brightness of flavour. The raw zucchini (courgette) 'noodles' make for a wonderfully light breakfast. You can blanch them if you prefer – place the spiralised zucchini in a colander in the sink and pour over boiling water from the kettle.

# Lemongrass pork 'noodle' bowl

1 stalk lemongrass, pale
section only
1 tablespoon peanut oil
1 tablespoon curry laksa
paste
400 g (14 oz) minced
(ground) pork
1 red capsicum (bell
pepper), chopped
1 teaspoon finely grated
fresh turmeric
1 red Asian shallot, finely
sliced
2 tablespoons fish sauce,
or to taste
1 tablespoon lime juice,
or to taste
1 teaspoon coconut sugar,
or to taste
handful coriander (cilantro)
leaves
handful mint leaves
2 zucchini (courgettes),
spiralised (see page 8)

**To serve**
lime cheeks
chopped roasted salted
peanuts
thinly sliced red chilli

Soak the lemongrass in boiling water for 20 seconds to soften, then chop finely and set aside.

Heat a wok or large frying pan over high heat. Add the oil and laksa paste and stir-fry for 30 seconds or until fragrant. Add the minced pork and stir-fry for 5–6 minutes until the pork is just cooked through. Add the capsicum, turmeric and lemongrass and stir-fry until the capsicum just starts to soften.

Add the shallot, fish sauce, lime juice and coconut sugar. Stir well and taste for balance. Add a little more of the seasonings if required. Remove from the heat and toss through the coriander and mint.

Serve the pork mixture into bowls with the spiralised zucchini. Top with lime cheeks, peanuts and chilli.

**Makes 4**

**Refined-sugar free | Dairy free | Gluten free | Grain free**

# Japanese miso bowl with pumpkin & spinach

200 g jap, kent or butternut
   pumpkin (squash)
1 handful baby spinach
   leaves
80 g (2¾ oz/¼ cup) white
   (shiro) miso paste, or to
   taste

**Dashi stock**
1 strip kombu seaweed
handful bonito
   (katsuobushi) flakes

**To serve**
roasted black sesame
   seeds
white sesame seeds

To make the dashi stock, pour 1 litre (34 fl oz/4 cups) water into a saucepan and add the kombu. Set aside to soak for 30 minutes. Bring just to the boil over medium heat then remove the kombu immediately. Add the bonito flakes and simmer for 2 minutes. Remove from the heat and set aside to steep for 5 minutes. Line a sieve with muslin (cheesecloth) or paper towel and strain the stock into a bowl. Discard the bonito (or you can use it once more to make a lighter stock) and return the stock to the saucepan.

Meanwhile, scoop out the seeds and carefully peel about half of the skin from the pumpkin, leaving the remaining skin in patches. Cut the pumpkin into bite-sized pieces and add to the stock. Bring to the boil and simmer, uncovered for 5–6 minutes or until the pumpkin is tender. Remove from the heat and stir in the spinach.

Combine the miso with a small amount of stock in a small bowl, stir gently with chopsticks then add it to the soup. Stir until combined. Traditionally, it is not recommended that the soup is boiled after adding the miso, but if you like your miso piping hot, you can reheat it gently.

Ladle the soup into bowls and serve immediately.

**Makes 4**

**Refined-sugar free | Vegan | Gluten free**

Leaving about half of the skin on the pumpkin (squash) adds a great bit of texture to the tender vegetable. If you are strapped for time, instead of making the stock from scratch, combine about 2 teaspoons dashi stock powder with 1 litre (34 fl oz/4 cups) water.

Savoury oats may seem a bit unusual, but once the runny egg yolk from your perfectly fried egg mingles with the slightly salty, creamy oats, you'll be an instant convert.

# Oats with egg & pickled carrot

120 g (4½ oz/1⅓ cups)
  rolled (traditional/
  porridge) oats
160 ml (5½ fl oz/⅔ cup)
  light chicken or vegetable
  stock
1 teaspoon peanut oil
4 free-range eggs

**Pickled carrot**

2 tablespoons white wine
  vinegar
1 teaspoon pure maple
  syrup
½ teaspoon fish sauce
1 carrot, julienned
½ small red onion, thinly
  sliced

**To serve**

finely sliced spring onion
  (scallions)
red chilli
roasted black sesame
  seeds

To make the pickled carrot, combine the vinegar, maple syrup and fish sauce in a bowl. Add the carrot and onion and mix well. Set aside to pickle, stirring occasionally, for at least 30 minutes. Drain before serving.

Combine the oats and stock with 625ml (21 fl oz/2½ cups) water in a heavy-based saucepan. Stir over low heat for about 5 minutes until the mixture comes to the boil, then simmer for 5–6 minutes, stirring occasionally, until thick and creamy. If necessary, thin with a little hot water to reach the consistency you like (I like my savoury oats a little thinner in texture than traditional oatmeal/porridge).

Meanwhile, heat the oil in a heavy-based frying pan over medium–high heat. Carefully break the eggs into the pan and cook for 2–2½ minutes until the whites are crispy around the edges, but the yolks are still runny (or until cooked to your liking). Carefully flip each of the eggs over, if you like, and remove from the heat.

Serve the oats into bowls and top each with an egg and pickled carrot, spring onion, chilli and a scattering of sesame seeds.

**Makes 4**

**Refined-sugar free | Dairy free**

*To make **vegetarian**, replace the fish sauce with soy sauce.*

# Smoked salmon salad bowl

1 ripe pear (skin on), finely
    sliced on a mandoline
1–2 lemons, cut into
    wedges
1 fennel bulb, fronds
    reserved, bulb finely
    sliced on a mandoline
4 baby radishes, finely
    sliced on a mandoline
extra-virgin olive oil, to
    drizzle
200 g (7 oz) thinly sliced
    smoked salmon
1 lime, segmented

## Crostini

1 garlic clove, cut in half
8 x 1 cm (½ in) slices
    baguette
1 tablespoon olive oil

## Herb labneh

125 g (4½ oz/½ cup) labneh
    (see page 79)
    or crème fraiche
2 tablespoons chopped
    herbs (such as parsley,
    tarragon and chives)

To make the crostini, preheat the oven to 160°C/320°F (fan-forced). Rub the cut sides of the garlic lightly over the bread slices. Brush the bread all over with olive oil and place on a baking tray. Bake for 15–20 minutes, turning after 10 minutes, until lightly golden and crisp.

For the herb labneh, combine the labneh or crème fraiche and herbs in a small bowl. Season lightly with salt and pepper. Set aside until required.

Place the pear in a large bowl and toss with a squeeze of lemon juice to prevent the pear from discolouring. Add the fennel and radish, squeeze over more lemon juice and add a glug of olive oil. Season with a little salt and pepper. Toss gently to combine.

Serve the salad between four large wide bowls and top with the smoked salmon, lime segments, a dollop or two of herb labneh and the crostini. Scatter with the reserved fennel fronds.

**Makes 4**

**Refined-sugar free**

*To make **gluten free**, omit the crostini.*

This is a lovely light breakfast dish that also makes for an elegant brunch. The crisp salad adds freshness and tang alongside luxurious smoked salmon and the irresistible crunch of the crostini.

These hot, smoky beans are the ultimate in hearty and warming breakfasts, especially when paired with creamy scrambled eggs and the spicy, moreish green rice.

# Smoky Mexican black bean bowl with green rice

1 tablespoon olive oil

1 leek, pale section finely sliced

1 tablespoon tomato paste (concentrated purée)

2 teaspoons smoked hot paprika

1 garlic clove, crushed

200 g (7 oz) tinned diced tomatoes

400 g (14 oz) tin black beans, drained and rinsed

20 g (¾ oz) butter

4 large free-range eggs

## Green rice

500 ml (17 fl oz/2 cups) vegetable or chicken stock

1 tablespoon pickled jalapeño slices

25 g (1 oz/½ cup) chopped coriander (cilantro) stems and leaves

2 teaspoons olive oil

150 g (5½ oz/¾ cup) brown wholegrain basmati rice

2 cloves garlic, crushed

## To serve

coriander (cilantro) leaves
shredded spring onion

To make the green rice, warm the stock and jalapeños in a small saucepan over low heat for 5 minutes. Stir in the coriander, set aside to cool slightly, then, using a hand-held blender, purée the stock mixture until smooth. Strain into a jug, using a spatula to press some of the green pulp through the strainer. Discard the remaining pulp. Heat the oil in a medium-sized heavy-based saucepan over medium heat and cook the rice and garlic, stirring for 1 minute or until fragrant. Add 330 ml (11 fl oz/1⅓ cups) of the jalapeño stock, bring to the boil, reduce the heat to low and then cook, covered for 25–30 minutes or until the stock has been absorbed and the rice is tender. Remove from the heat and stand for 10 minutes, covered.

Meanwhile, heat the oil in a large non-stick frying pan over medium–low heat. Add the leek and cook, stirring occasionally, for 8–10 minutes until tender. Add the tomato paste, paprika and garlic, increase the heat to medium and cook, stirring, for about 1 minute or until fragrant. Stir in the tinned tomato, beans and ½ cup (125 ml) water, bring to the boil, reduce the heat and simmer for 10–15 minutes or until thickened. Remove from the heat and cover to keep warm.

While the rice is resting, heat the butter in a large heavy-based frying pan over medium heat. Whisk the eggs in a bowl with 60 ml (2 fl oz/¼ cup) water and a pinch of salt, making sure the salt has a chance to dissolve. When the butter is foaming, add the egg mixture to the pan. Gently move the egg around the pan with a spatula until scrambled to your liking. When the egg is almost set, remove from the heat.

Serve the rice into bowls and top with the smoky beans and scrambled egg. Finish with coriander and spring onion.

**Makes 4**

**Refined-sugar free | Vegetarian | Gluten free**

# Turkish breakfast bowl with baked ricotta

1 teaspoon pul biber (Turkish crushed chilli) or crushed chilli flakes

450 g (1 lb) firm fresh ricotta

2 free-range eggs

3 spring onions (scallions), finely chopped

2 vine-ripened tomatoes, sliced

2 Lebanese cucumbers, sliced

2 hard-boiled eggs, peeled and halved

**To serve**

black and green olives

baby spinach or rocket leaves

sliced toasted Turkish bread

extra-virgin olive oil

Preheat the oven to 160°C/320°F (fan-forced). Lightly grease a shallow 500 ml (17 fl oz/2 cup) ovenproof baking dish with olive oil spray. Sprinkle the base with the crushed chilli.

Mash the ricotta in a bowl using a fork. Add the egg and spring onion and mix well. Season lightly with salt and pepper. Spoon the mixture into the prepared dish, smooth the surface and bake for 35–40 minutes or until puffed, golden and set in the centre. Set aside for 10 minutes to settle.

Loosen the edges of the baked ricotta and turn out onto a cutting board or plate. The baked ricotta may be served warm or cold. Cover and store in the refrigerator for up to 3 days if not using straight away.

Cut the ricotta into wedges and serve into large shallow bowls. Add the tomato, cucumber and egg. Serve with olives, spinach leaves, Turkish bread slices and drizzle with olive oil.

**Makes 4**

**Refined-sugar free | Vegetarian**

This tasty baked ricotta can be eaten warm, not long out of the oven, but it's is equally enjoyable served cool. It can be made ahead of time, or indeed the day before, in which case this breakfast is pretty quick to assemble. If you pop your eggs on to cook first up, they'll be done by the time you've arranged everything else.

This is a hearty, yet light and nutritious breakfast bowl that will get your day off to a flying start. The freshness of the coriander (cilantro) quinoa, the toasty corn, crunchy tortilla chips and creamy guacamole make for a killer combination.

# Coriander quinoa & corn bowl with tortilla chips

2 corn cobs, husks and silk discarded
2 teaspoons olive oil
50 g (1¾ oz) cotija cheese or feta, crumbled
microherbs, to serve

## Coriander quinoa

200 g (7 oz/1 cup) red and white quinoa, rinsed
large handful coriander (cilantro) leaves
1 spring onion (scallion), chopped
zest and juice of 1 lime
1 tablespoon olive oil

## Tortilla chips

2 small flour tortillas
2 teaspoons olive oil

## Guacamole

1 avocado, stone removed
1 small tomato, chopped
½ small red onion, finely chopped
2 tablespoons natural yoghurt
lime juice, to taste
1 teaspoon chopped chipotle chilli in adobo sauce (optional)

To make the coriander quinoa, put the quinoa and 500 ml (17 fl oz/ 2 cups) water in a large saucepan and bring to the boil over medium heat. Cover, reduce the heat to low and simmer for 10–12 minutes or until most, if not all, of the water has evaporated and the grains are tender. Remove from the heat, drain if required and transfer to a large bowl to cool slightly. Stir in the coriander, spring onion, lime zest and juice and olive oil. Season with salt and pepper and set aside until required. The quinoa may be served warm or cool.

Meanwhile, heat a chargrill pan over high heat. Rub the corn lightly with the olive oil, sprinkle with a little salt and chargrill for 12–15 minutes, turning occasionally, until charred and cooked. Remove from heat and set aside to cool slightly. Cut each cob into six slices.

For the tortilla chips, preheat the oven to 160°C/320°F (fan-forced). Brush the tortillas lightly on both sides with the olive oil and cut into long thin triangles. Place on an oven tray and bake, turning halfway through, for 8–10 minutes or until lightly browned and crisp. Remove from the oven and cool on the tray.

To make the guacamole, cut the avocado into cubes and place in a bowl. Roughly mash the avocado with a fork, being careful to retain some texture. Stir in the tomato, onion, yoghurt and lime juice. Season with salt and pepper, and, if you like, stir in the chipotle chilli in adobo sauce.

Serve the quinoa into bowls and top with the corn, tortilla chips and guacamole. Scatter with the cheese and microherbs.

**Makes 4**

**Refined-sugar free | Vegetarian**

*To make **gluten free**, omit the tortillas, or use corn tortillas instead.*

# Index

# Dietary index

## Vegan

## Dairy free

## Gluten free

## Grain free

# Thanks

*Note: The majority of recipes in the book are refined-sugar free and vegetarian so have not been specified here. Most of the recipes are easy to adapt to suit your dietary needs, please see the recipe pages for suggested variations.*

Thank you ever so much Paul McNally and Smith Street Books for giving me the opportunity to create this array of beautiful and nutritious recipes. Thank you to Hannah Koelmeyer for your editing expertise; it is always a pleasure to work with you.

Producing a cookbook is always such a team effort. Thank you for the beautiful design work Michelle Mackintosh and Heather Menzies, the gorgeous images Chris Middleton and your splendid styling Vicki Valsamis. Jemima Good, huge thanks to you for getting us through the photo shoot – your dedication and passion will take you far - whichever direction you choose.

None of this would be possible without the tireless support of my wonderful husband Kaine and the constant enthusiasm of our boys. Love you.

To my dearest mum, Doreen, thank you always for your unwavering support and allowing us into your home for the shoot. We were lucky to have Cali the pooch standing guard! And, to my wider family and wonderful friends, who are always so encouraging.

I am so fortunate to be able to do this thing I love so much. I know I'm not saving the world, but hopefully some of my recipes will make some people happy – either because they have discovered something new, enjoyed the recipe themselves, or have nourished others with their lovingly created breakfast bowl and felt the love reflected back to them.

ISBN: 978-1-925418-26-2

CIP data is available from the National Library of Australia.

Publisher: Paul McNally
Project editor: Hannah Koelmeyer, Tusk studio
Design concept: Michelle Mackintosh
Design layout: Heather Menzies, Studio31 Graphics
Photography: Chris Middleton
Food styling: Vicki Valsamis
Food preparation: Caroline Griffiths & Jemima Good

Printed & bound in China by C&C Offset Printing Co., Ltd.

Book 21
10 9 8 7 6 5 4 3 2 1